ESSENTIAL [

9-YEAR-OLD NEEDS TO KNOW

A Guide to Help Young Boys and Girls Succeed in Life.

AUTHOR
DIANE POPE

Copyright Page

Title: Essential Life Skills Every 9-Year-Old Needs to Know

Sub Title: A Guide to Help Young Boys and Girls Succeed in Life

Author: Diane Pope

Published by Skilled Fun

SKILLED FUN

For permission requests, contact the publisher:

Skilled Fun

401 Ryland Street,

Suite 200-A,

Reno, NV, 89502,

USA

ISBN: 979-8-89256-005-4

Printed in USA

CONTENTS

SPECIAL BONUS

Want this bonus book for free?

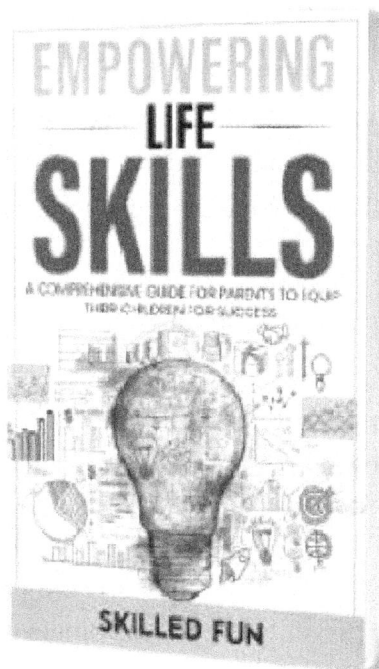

BONUS

EMPOWERING LIFE SKILLS

A COMPREHENSIVE GUIDE FOR PARENTS TO EQUIP THEIR CHILDREN FOR SUCCESS

FREE

SKILLED FUN

SKILLS and be the first to claim a free download of our upcoming releases.

Scan the QR CODE

Join Today!

INTRODUCTION

A re you ready to embark on a journey where you'll learn super cool secrets about growing up and being awesome at it?

Life skills are like your superhero toolkit, packed with amazing powers to help you navigate this exciting ride called life. Just like a hero needs their gadgets and wisdom, you too can equip yourself with the essential skills to conquer daily challenges and become a real-life superstar!

In this book, we'll discover the secrets of being kind, sharing, staying organized, listening, and so much more. It's like uncovering hidden treasure and discovering the keys to unlock a world of awesomeness.

We'll learn how sharing a smile or lending a helping hand can brighten someone's day and make the world a better place. Imagine having the power to spread happiness wherever you go — pretty cool, right? Plus, being a great listener means you can understand others better and be an amazing friend. These skills will make you a real hero in the eyes of the people you care about.

And let's not forget the mighty power of staying organized! It's like having a secret spell that helps you find your stuff and manage your time wisely. With a little practice, you'll become a master organizer, and you'll see how much smoother everything runs. Are you ready to unlock these incredible abilities and become the ultimate champion of life skills? Let's dive into the adventure and uncover the magic that's waiting for you!

So, fasten your seatbelt and get ready for an adventure that will transform you into a life skills champion. Let's dive in and make this journey one for the storybooks!

CHAPTER 1

EMBARKING ON THE EPIC ADVENTURE

Now, you are not eight years old anymore, and you know so much more than what we began with. We are not only on a journey but on a ladder that will keep on taking us on amazing adventures. So, what is the first adventure? What if I tell you the first stop is not a fun adventure, but the idea that everything can be an adventure you can enjoy, and learn new and exciting things from? It's about seeing the world around us as a big adventure playground, filled with hidden treasures of learning and fun!

Imagine you have a super-duper adventure lens, just like the lens on binoculars. When you put it on, ordinary stuff becomes EXTRAORDINARY! You see, helping others is like putting on those adventure lenses. When you help, it's like finding secret passages in a video game. You discover new paths and cool surprises.

Helping others is like being a kind superhero. Every small act of kindness is like your superpower. It's like having a magical cape that spreads happiness wherever you go. Remember when you shared your snacks with a friend or helped a classmate with their homework? Yep, that's the adventure we're talking about...

You're not just living life; you're turning it into a grand adventure. And guess what? The more you adventure with kindness, the more exciting life becomes. Every homework, every bicycle ride, and every video game becomes a game of its own. Our adventure today isn't about pirates or rocket ships—it's about finding excitement in everything around us. Imagine the world as a giant playground, full of exciting games and awesome discoveries.

Think of your day like a treasure map. Every activity, every moment, is a new spot on the map. And guess what? There's a hidden treasure in each spot. The treasure is all the cool stuff you can learn and enjoy. For example, when you open a book, it's like digging for buried treasure. Each page you read uncovers shiny jewels of knowledge and imagination. You can go on daring adventures, solve mysterious puzzles, and meet fascinating characters—all through the magic of reading!

Ever tried solving a puzzle or cracking a secret code? Learning new things is like cracking a code! It's a brain puzzle, and each piece you figure out brings you closer to unveiling the hidden picture of knowledge. Remember the time you planted a seed and watched it grow into a plant? Learning is a bit like that too! Each bit of knowledge you absorb is a tiny seed. As you learn and explore, those seeds grow into big, beautiful gardens of understanding.

Everyone gets tired of having so many questions or even answering too many questions. But what if we start thinking about

4

each question as a treasure? Questions are like magical keys that unlock doors to amazing places. The more questions you ask, the more doors you can open, and the more adventures you can have.

So, my incredible friend, every day is a chance for a new adventure. There's excitement in learning how a caterpillar becomes a butterfly, in discovering new words, and in understanding why the sky changes colors at sunset. The world is full of wonder waiting for you to explore.

I know sometimes days get boring, and it becomes hard to be excited about the same thing every day: the same school, same friends, and the same dinners with family. But what actually makes me sad is how people, whether they're only nine like you or a grownup, stop enjoying things. We have to learn to enjoy and learn from everything around us. A special "window" that allows us to make each moment exciting. Let me show you how:

BORING	FUN!
Dinner every night.	Family time to play Monopoly, or even FIFA together!
Wake up every morning to go to school.	Let's go meet our friends and learn exciting new facts.
Do we want to play with the same friends again?	Let's come up with exciting new games together!
Homework!!!	I can call my friends because this homework seems too much; I'm sure we can do it better together and enjoy it.

It is all about making a choice to enjoy every day and turning every new thing into a challenge that you know you can solve. All you need is you. Because you are always your own superhero!

CHAPTER 2

QUEST FOR THE HIDDEN TREASURES OF GOALS

A goal is something you want to achieve. It's like a target you aim for, whether it's learning a new skill, getting better at a game, or acing a school project. Goals give you a sense of purpose and direction. Imagine your goals as secret islands waiting to be discovered. Each island holds a treasure chest of achievements. To begin your quest, create a "goal treasure map." Draw islands and name them with exciting titles like "Reading Adventure Island" or "Math Mastery Mountain."

Just like a pirate faces storms at sea, you might encounter challenges on your journey toward your goals. Don't let these deter you. Adjust your sails, stay determined, and keep moving forward. Challenges make the journey more exciting. Every step you take towards your goals is like exploring a new territory and discovering uncharted lands. Just as a pirate navigates the seas to reach a hidden island, you will navigate your journey by following the path you've set in your "goal treasure map."

Remember, each goal you accomplish is a triumph — a treasure chest of achievements. It's proof that you set your sights on something, worked hard, and made it happen. The feeling of achieving a goal is like finding a precious gem or gold doubloon — it's priceless and makes the journey worthwhile.

Goals can be both short-term and long-term. Short-term goals are like little islands you can reach quickly. They can be achieved in a few days or weeks. Long-term goals are like distant lands that take more time and effort to reach. Both types of goals are important in your quest for hidden treasures. I have a very interesting story about such adventurers on an island like this...

Once upon a time in the land of "Adventureville," there lived a group of young adventurers who loved exploring and learning new things. They were always on the lookout for exciting quests. One sunny morning, the adventurers gathered in the town square, where Captain Curious, the wisest of them all, had a special announcement.

"Ahoy, young adventurers! Today, we're setting sail on a magnificent journey — the "Quest for the Hidden Treasures of Goals." Just like a treasure hunt, we'll learn how to set goals and work towards them," boomed Captain Curious. The adventurers gathered around in anticipation, eager to learn and embark on this new adventure.

"Let's start with understanding what a 'goal' is," explained Captain Curious. "A goal is like a treasure you want to find or an adventure you want to complete. It's something you aim for and work to achieve."

Their eyes sparkled with curiosity. Each adventurer was ready to set sail on this knowledge-filled voyage. "Our first step is to create a treasure map for our goals," said Captain Curious, holding up a big piece of paper. "On this map, we'll mark the places we want to reach — the goals we want to achieve."

The adventurers received their own pieces of paper and colorful pens to draw their maps. "Now, let's name our 'goal islands,'" continued Captain Curious. "Give them exciting names like 'Learn-a-Lot Island' or 'Adventureland Mountain.' The names will keep us excited about reaching our goals!"

The adventurers got to work, scribbling and naming their islands. They grinned as their imagination sailed to far-off lands. "Now, let's fill our treasure chests with goals for each island," Captain Curious exclaimed. "What would you like to achieve on each island? Think of small, achievable steps that will lead you to your treasure!" The adventurers filled their islands with goals like "Read Ten Books" and "Learn to Ride a Bicycle." Each goal was a step toward their treasure.

"A good adventurer always plans the journey," Captain Curious reminded them. "Let's make our 'adventure plans' — a step-by-step guide to reach our goals. X marks the spots where our treasure chests, our achievements, will be." The adventurers carefully outlined their adventure plans, connecting their steps to the treasure spots.

As the day went on, the adventurers felt a surge of excitement. Their "Quest for the Hidden Treasures of Goals" had just begun.

Each step they took was like following a trail, leading them to their precious treasures. At the end of the day, they gathered once more in the town square, their maps and plans ready. Captain Curious beamed with pride at their enthusiasm.

"Young adventurers, you've set sail on a remarkable journey today," Captain Curious said, clapping his hands. "Remember, every step you take is a step closer to your treasure. Celebrate your achievements and keep exploring."

The adventurers cheered, ready to continue their adventure, eager to uncover the treasures of their goals. With their maps in hand and hearts full of determination, they knew they were on the most exciting journey of their lives—the "Quest for the Hidden Treasures of Goals."

This story is a special example of how fun it is to have goals and try to achieve them. There is also another very important thing you have to remember, no matter what. The best thing you can do after having goals is to try really hard to make them come true, but never beat yourself down for not achieving them after one try. Everything happens in its own great time. Sometimes things happen fast, and sometimes great things take time. The important thing is finding out what you truly love and then following your heart.

Something tells me you are smart enough to know all of that already!

CHAPTER 3

CASTLE OF CONFIDENCE AND THE POWER OF POSITIVITY

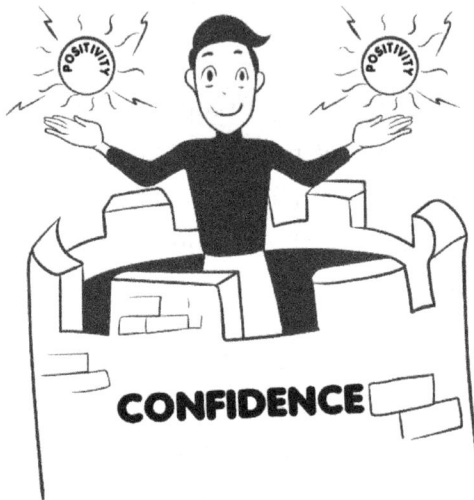

I know some days are just a bummer. Like straight up the worst days of your life. Like the days you spent doing your homework, and finally when it was time to give it to your teacher, you kept the wrong file in your bag. Or the time you planned an awesome birthday party at a water park and invited all your friends. But it started to rain out of nowhere. Now your party is ruined and so is your mood. It is hard to stay positive on days like that. Everything seems so dull and wrong. I don't blame you. I feel like that sometimes too. Everyone does.

But here's a secret that I've learned on my adventures — it's like finding a hidden treasure. You have the power to turn things around, even on the darkest of days. Imagine this power as a castle, strong and huge. Let's call it the Castle of Confidence. Inside this castle, you'll discover the tools and magical spells to conquer those tough days and emerge victorious. This specific magic is positivity. What is positivity? Just being able to find good in everything, no matter how bad something is.

First, let's talk about confidence. It's like wearing a suit of armor that protects you from negativity. When you believe in yourself, even the darkest clouds can't dampen your spirit. Think of a time when you aced a test or scored a goal. That feeling of "I can do it" is your armor, and you should wear it proudly. Every adventure in life needs a dose of positivity. It's like the sunshine that lights up your day, even when it's stormy. Positive thoughts and a smile can be your best friends. Even when things don't go as planned, finding a little bit of good in a bad situation is like finding a bright lamp — it guides you through the tough times.

Now, let me tell you a magical secret spell: "I CAN." These two words have immense power. When you say, "I CAN," it's like unlocking a treasure chest of possibilities. It's the key to the Castle of Confidence. Believe in yourself, say "I CAN," and watch the doors of opportunity swing open. Positivity is also about embracing a "can-do" attitude. It's like having a magical spell that turns "I can't" into "I can." Believe that you can overcome any challenge, and that you can achieve your dreams. With positivity as your wand, you can create a world of endless possibilities.

Life is an epic adventure, and you are the hero of your story. In every story, the hero faces challenges, but what makes them true heroes is their courage to overcome those challenges. Believe that you are a hero, facing each day with courage and a positive spirit.

The more you practice positivity, the more it becomes a natural part of you. It's like a beautiful garden that you nurture daily. Water it with happy thoughts, the sunlight of hope, and the fertilizer of kindness. Soon, you'll have a garden blooming with positivity, attracting butterflies of joy and peace.

You might be thinking, "But how can I find this Castle of Confidence and learn the Power of Positivity?" Well, the secret is— it's within you. Yes, right in your heart and mind. You can build this castle with your thoughts, your beliefs, and your actions. It's a castle built with self-belief, kindness, resilience, and a sprinkle of laughter.

In this castle, there's a special room filled with mirrors. These aren't ordinary mirrors; they show you your strengths and talents. When you look into them, you see all the amazing things about yourself—the things that make you special. Believe in these reflections, for they are the true you. Every day is a new page of your adventure book. You get to write the story, and the Castle of Confidence and the Power of Positivity is your trusted pen.

I want you to imagine yourself as an artist, painting the canvas of your life with vibrant colors. Confidence and positivity are the brushes you use to create a masterpiece. Each stroke of confidence adds strength to your creation, while every splash of positivity adds brightness and joy. Have you ever noticed how laughter can light up a room? Because it is time you do. It's like a magical potion that can turn a dull moment into a cheerful one. Laughter is a treasure chest in the Castle of Confidence. When you laugh, it's as if you've found a hidden gem, making you feel lighter and happier.

Sometimes, even in the Castle of Confidence, we face tough challenges. It's like a dragon protecting its treasure. But you, brave adventurer, can face these dragons with the sword of determination. Every swing of this sword is a step towards conquering your fears and doubts. Inside the castle, there's a magical garden where kind words and acts of kindness grow. Just like planting seeds, when you spread kindness, it blossoms into a beautiful garden of friendships and connections. The more you nurture it, the more vibrant and lovely your world becomes.

In the heart of the Castle of Confidence lies a chamber of dreams. This is where you dream big, like a dragon spreading its wings. Your dreams are the treasures you seek, and the castle is the place where you plan your quest to achieve them. Believe in your dreams, and they will become the guiding stars of your adventure.

Just like a knight in shining armor, your kindness and compassion can rescue others in need. It's like having a magical shield that protects and uplifts those around you. Remember, being kind not only brightens someone else's day but fills your heart with warmth and happiness too.

As you spend every day, you'll have moments that will challenge your confidence and positivity. It's okay to have moments of doubt or sadness — it's a part of being human. Think of these moments as cloudy days in your adventure. But just as the sun always shines after a storm, your inner sunshine will break through the clouds, bringing hope and renewal. Now, my brave adventurer, it's time to unlock the full potential of the Castle of Confidence using the Power of Positivity. All you have to do is be brave, believe in your dreams, and sprinkle kindness. Let this castle be your safe place, a place where you can always find the courage to win everything.

Believe in yourself. You are stronger and more capable than you may ever realize.

CHAPTER 4

EMOTION AVENGERS: DEFEATING THE DARK EMOTION MONSTERS

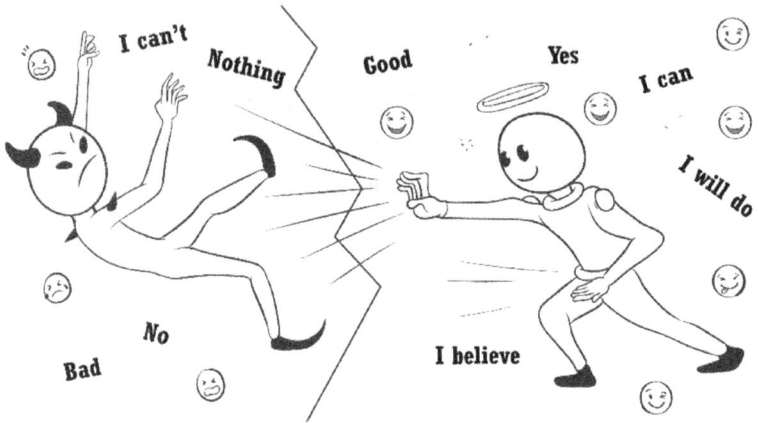

Feelings are like the colors of your heart. Just like you have a favorite crayon, you might have a favorite feeling too. Sometimes, you feel really happy, just like when you see your favorite toy. Other times, you might feel a bit sad, like when your friend has to go home after a fun playdate. Imagine your heart like a special place with lots of rooms. Each feeling gets its own room, and sometimes, more than one feeling can be in your heart at the same time. It's a little like having guests over for a party—some guests like to dance and be cheerful, while others might sit quietly and watch.

Feeling sad is when you feel a bit low, like when it's a rainy day, and you can't go out to play. It's totally normal to feel sad sometimes, and everyone feels this way every now and then. The good news is that just like the rain eventually stops, sadness goes away too. Anger is a strong feeling that might make you feel like a volcano about to erupt. Maybe you feel this way when things don't go your way, or when you're frustrated. It's okay to feel angry, but what's important is how we handle it. Taking deep breaths and talking about what's bothering you can help cool down the angry flames.

Being scared is like feeling a little shaky, like when you see a big, dark cave. It's okay to feel scared — it's your body's way of being cautious. Sometimes, learning more about what scares you can make it feel less scary. Just like having a flashlight in a dark cave, understanding can make things brighter. Happiness is like a burst of sunshine! It's that amazing feeling when everything is just right. Maybe it's a fun game with friends, a delicious ice cream, or a hug from someone you love. Feeling happy is like having a pocket full of joy, and you can sprinkle that joy on others too.

Just like superheroes have their special tools and powers, we have our own to manage our feelings. Taking deep breaths, talking to someone we trust, understanding how others feel, and finding the bright side of things are our superpowers. With these, we can conquer any challenge that comes our way. Becoming an Emotion Avenger means learning about our feelings, understanding them, and using our superpowers to make the world around us a better and happier place.

Being an Emotion Avenger means we get to choose how we color our world with feelings. Sometimes, it's fun to mix colors too! For instance, combining happiness with a sprinkle of kindness can make a beautiful shade of joy. Just like mixing yellow and blue makes green, mixing our feelings can create something new and wonderful. Understanding how others might be feeling is like having a secret map to their hearts. It helps us be kinder and more caring. If you notice a friend feeling down, you can share your colors of happiness to brighten their day. Together, we can create a rainbow of emotions, making the world a happier and brighter place.

It's essential to remember that just like the weather, our feelings can change. Today might be a bit cloudy, but tomorrow could be sunny and bright. The key is to embrace each feeling and know that it's a part of the beautiful you. As we go on this adventure of understanding feelings, let's remember our special powers as Emotion Avengers. When we take deep breaths and stay calm, we can handle any storm of emotions that might come our way. Talking to someone we trust helps us understand our feelings better, like having a helpful guide on our journey.

Each day is a new page in our emotions' adventure book. We get to write the story with the colors of our hearts. Let's choose to fill it with love, joy, kindness, and all the amazing feelings that make our adventure extraordinary.

CHAPTER 5

EXPRESS-O-METER: BREWING THE WORDS OF EMOTION

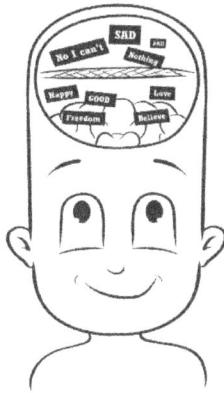

So, understanding emotions is the buzz, but it is not just about knowing and understanding them. It is also about learning to properly use them. It's like when you're playing with your favorite toys and each toy makes you feel a different way — happy, excited, or sometimes even a little shy.

Understanding these feelings is like knowing the names of your toys. Just like knowing that your teddy bear is called "Fluffy," or your toy car is "Speedy," understanding feelings helps you name what's going on inside you.

Imagine feelings are like colors in a magical box of crayons. You have bright yellows, blues, and greens. Sometimes you feel as warm as a sunny yellow and sometimes as cool as a calm blue. Just like colors, feelings are part of our everyday adventure. But wait, there's more! It's not just about knowing the colors; it's about using them to paint a beautiful picture. That's where our "Express-O-Meter" comes in. It's like a special tool that helps us pick the right crayons (or feelings) for the right picture (or situation).

First on our colorful feelings palette is "happy." Happy is like a sunny day with a sky full of smiles. It's when you get your favorite snack or when you're playing with friends. Happy is a super-duper, mega-awesome feeling. Imagine you're at a party with all your best buddies, and there's your favorite game to play! Your face lights up with a big smile, and you feel like doing a happy dance. That's the happy feeling, like a burst of sunshine inside you.

How to communicate happy: You can say, "Wow, I'm really happy today because I get to play with all of you!"

Now what about the opposite of happy? That's sad. Sad is like a raincloud that comes and goes. Maybe you dropped your ice cream, or perhaps your best friend had to leave. Feeling sad is like having a tiny rainstorm in your heart. It's okay to feel sad because it's like a gentle rain that helps the flowers grow. It is like imagining that you're playing with your toys, and suddenly your favorite toy breaks. You might feel a little teary-eyed and down. That's feeling sad, like a raincloud passing through your sunny day.

Now what about how to communicate sadness: You can say, "I'm feeling a bit sad right now because my toy broke. Can we talk about it?"

And what happens when we are so happy that we cannot even wait for something to happen? That is called excitement. Excited is like fireworks of energy inside you. It's when you're going to your favorite amusement park or when you're about to open a special surprise gift. Excited is like a bunch of colorful fireworks lighting up the night sky. I need you to imagine something for me: you've been waiting for weeks, and now you're about to go to the amusement park! You can't help but bounce around and smile from ear to ear. That's the excited feeling, like a party of bubbles inside you.

How to communicate being excited? You can say, "I'm so excited about our adventure today! It's going to be amazing!"

Oh, here comes "angry"!

Being "angry" is like a firecracker that's popped. It's when things don't go the way you want, and you feel a bit like a volcano about to erupt. Feeling angry is like having a strong and fiery feeling, wanting things to be fair and right. I want you to think that you're playing a game, and someone breaks the rules or takes your turn. You might feel a rush of heat and frustration, like a firecracker sizzling and popping. That's feeling angry, like a spark of energy that says, "Hey, that's not fair!"

How to communicate anger, you ask? You can say, "I'm feeling upset because I wanted a turn too. Let's take turns, so it's fair for everyone."

But you know the most important emotion that we need to remind ourselves of quite a bit. When you are too angry, so happy, or too sad. Calmness!

Calm is like a quiet, peaceful lake. It's when you're sitting in a cozy spot with a good book or watching the trees sway gently. Calm is like a soft and gentle feeling that makes you feel relaxed and at ease. Close your eyes and imagine you're sitting by a lake, feeling the gentle breeze on your skin, and listening to the water softly lapping against the shore. That's feeling calm, like a peaceful lake inside you.

But what about how to communicate calmly? You can say, "Taking a deep breath helps me feel calm and relaxed. Let's take a moment to breathe together."

But our adventure in understanding feelings doesn't stop there. Let's hop on another colorful path and discover even more about these amazing emotions. I need you to understand that it is all hard work and it takes time to learn…

Imagine feelings are like ingredients for a recipe. Just like you need the right ingredients to make a tasty cake, you need the right mix of feelings to make your day awesome. It's like having a special potion where you blend different feelings to create a magical brew.

Let's mix "happy" with "excited." It's like adding extra sprinkles to your ice cream. When you're excited about a school play, and you're happy because your friends are watching, it's a double scoop of pure joy. Imagine being gifted your favorite toy before your birthday. That would make you so so happy, right?

How to communicate excited and happy: You can say, "I'm super excited and happy about the play today! It's going to be so much fun!" But what about when you are just not that excited? Let's try mixing "calm" with "happy." It's like the quiet before a happy dance. Picture a cozy day at home with your favorite book, feeling so content and happy — it's a warm and peaceful kind of happiness!

How to communicate calmly and happily? Well, you can try saying, "Snuggling up with my book makes me feel calm and happy. It's my favorite thing to do on a rainy day."

How about blending "angry" with "sad"? It's like mixing storm clouds and raindrops. Maybe you're angry because your sandcastle got knocked down, and you're sad because it was your masterpiece. It's a mix of frustration and disappointment. That is when you have to take a step back and say, "I felt both angry and sad when my sandcastle got knocked down. It took a lot of hard work, and it made me upset."

Now, let's move on to "happy" and "calm" together. It's like a gentle breeze on a sunny day. Imagine you're in a beautiful garden, the sun is shining, and you're playing with your favorite pet. You feel a peaceful kind of happiness. This is where you can say, "Playing with my puppy in the garden makes me feel happy and calm. It's like my heart is smiling."

Mixing emotions is like being a wizard, brewing a magical potion with just the right ingredients. Just like a wizard knows the perfect combination of ingredients for a spell, you can learn to mix your feelings for a magical day.

So don't worry about when you don't get it right on the first day... take time and master the best way to learn to express and say how you feel out loud.

CHAPTER 6

EMPATHY: THE MAGIC POTION OF UNDERSTANDING

Imagine empathy like a magical potion, shimmering in a beautiful bottle. When you pour this potion into your heart, you suddenly understand how others are feeling. It's like having a magical mirror that reflects their emotions. To truly grasp empathy, let's think about being in someone else's shoes. Imagine your friend lost their favorite toy. They might feel sad and frustrated. How would you feel if you lost your favorite toy? That's the magic of empathy—you share their feelings.

Empathy isn't just about understanding the good feelings like happiness; it's also about understanding the tough feelings like sadness, anger, or fear. It's like having a map that helps you navigate the land of emotions. I want you to think of everyone who feels scared to be your friend. That is why I want you to imagine your friend is scared of the dark. They tremble and worry about what might be lurking in the shadows. You can offer them comfort and support because you understand how they feel, just like a warm, comforting potion.

How to show empathy: You can say, "I understand that the dark can be scary. I'm here for you, and we can face it together."

Empathy is a very strong word. It isn't about having all the answers or making everything okay. It's about being there, lending an ear, and offering a hug when someone needs it. It's like sprinkling a dash of kindness and understanding into the magic potion. So I want you to take a trip into the forest of friendship with me, where empathy is our guiding star. Imagine your friend is feeling left out, like a lone leaf on a tree. They might feel lonely and sad. Putting yourself in their shoes lets you understand and be there for them.

Imagine telling someone who is having a tough time, "I can imagine feeling left out is tough. How about we include you in our game?" It is not much, but making them feel heard and looked after can do a lot for someone in a bad situation. Empathy is also a bit like being a detective. You pay close attention to the clues—facial expressions, body language, and words—to understand what someone is feeling. It's like having a magical magnifying glass that helps you see beyond words.

Now, let's journey to the kingdom of family. Your little brother is upset because he can't find his favorite toy. You know how much he loves that toy. It's like sharing his sadness and frustration, making him feel less alone. But how do you show empathy to your family? You can say, "I know how much you love your toy. Let's search together, and I'm sure we'll find it."

Empathy is a kind of magic that makes the world a better place. It helps us connect with people, share their feelings, and support them through the ups and downs of life. It's like a never-ending potion of kindness and understanding.

Once you understand this, empathy is like a bridge that helps us cross over to someone else's world of emotions. If your friend is feeling worried about a big test, you can cross that empathy bridge and tell them, "I know tests can be nerve-wracking. You've got this!" It's like being a bridge-builder of understanding and comfort. So, you can say to someone who is super stressed before a very important test, "I remember feeling nervous before a test, too. Take a deep breath and do your best. You're capable and smart." See, it makes them feel happy and confident at the same time. You did not even have to do anything.

Empathy is not just about words; it's about actions too. Imagine your classmate is struggling with carrying heavy books. You offer to help, feeling the weight of their burden, just like carrying it yourself. It's like lending a helping hand and lightening their load. Just say, "I see those books are heavy. Let me help you carry them to the classroom."

And like I told you before. Making someone feel understood is so important. So, understanding becomes a very big part of empathy. Do you have a cousin? You like them. You grew up with them, too. But once you realize they're sad about something, you want them to feel better, right? Your cousin is upset because they can't visit their grandparents. You know how much they miss them. It's like sailing the seas of longing together, supporting them through the waves of sadness.

Start by saying, "I can see how much you miss Grandma and Grandpa. Let's plan a special video call with them."

Empathy can also be like a cozy blanket on a chilly day. Imagine your friend isn't feeling well. You can comfort them, saying, "I know being sick isn't fun. I'm here for you." It's like wrapping them in a warm embrace of caring and concern. Telling a sick friend that it's okay to not feel your best, and it takes time to get well can be so reassuring for them.

Now, let's unlock the magical power of empathy at school. Your classmate is struggling with a difficult math problem. Instead of teasing or showing off, you offer to explain, feeling their confusion like your own. It's like being a math wizard, helping them on their learning quest. Empathy is like a chain of kindness that links us all. When we show empathy, it inspires others to do the same. It's like spreading joyful ripples in a pond, reaching every corner with understanding and love. Thus, empathy also helps us be kinder and more patient. Picture a friend who's struggling to ride a bike. Instead of getting frustrated, you remember when you had a hard time, too. It's like a gentle breeze of understanding that helps them keep trying.

Empathy makes us true heroes, fighting for understanding and kindness. It's like having a shield of compassion that protects others from feeling alone. The more we practice empathy, the more we spread love and create a world where everyone feels valued.

CHAPTER 7

FRIENDSHIP TALK: CRAFTING KIND CONVERSATIONS

Making friends is never the hard part. I know this might seem kind of weird to say. As awesome as getting a new great friend is, it is harder to keep friends with them, especially when you do not know how to be kind, helpful, and understanding. Imagine you have a magical wand, and when you speak with kindness, you can sprinkle magic dust all around, making everyone feel happy and special. It's like being a wizard of good words!

First off, using kind words is like sharing your favorite treats. Imagine telling your friend, "You're awesome!" It's like giving them a cookie of kindness that makes them smile. One day, Tim was playing with his friend, Lily. He looked at Lily and said, "You're an amazing friend!" Lily's face lit up like a happy sun. Using kind words made their playtime even more fun and exciting.

Now, let's jump into the land of listening. Listening is like being a detective on a treasure hunt! When your friend tells you about their adventures, listen carefully with your magical ears. It's like being the best audience for their story. I want you to pretend to be nine-year-old Mia. In a cozy park, Mia sat with her friend Jake. Jake told her all about his new bike adventure. Mia listened closely, nodding, and saying, "Wow, that sounds like so much fun! Tell me more." Jake felt like a biking champion, and they laughed and talked for hours.

Next, we're off to the Kingdom of "Thank You." Saying "thank you" is like sending out friendly invitations to a party! When your friend shares something or helps you, saying thank you makes them feel extra special.

After a playdate, Emma hugged her friend, Noah, and said, "Thanks a bunch for sharing your toys!" Noah grinned and felt happy because he knew his friend appreciated his kindness.

Our adventure continues to the land of "I'm Sorry." Saying sorry is like using a magic eraser to fix little mistakes. Imagine if you accidentally bumped into your friend. Saying sorry helps to make things right and keeps your friendship strong. Here, we can use the story of little Max. One day, Max accidentally knocked over Lily's tower of blocks. He quickly said, "I'm sorry, Lily. It was an accident." Lily smiled and said, "It's okay, Max. Let's rebuild it together!"

As our journey sails, we arrive at the sea of "Excuse Me." Saying "excuse me" is like having a magic feather that helps your words float gently. It's a polite way to grab someone's attention and talk nicely. In a bustling classroom, Ethan raised his hand and said, "Excuse me, can I borrow a pencil, please?" The teacher smiled and handed him a pencil. Using "excuse me" made everything go smoothly.

Ethan was not just good at saying excuse me; I will tell you a little story about this kind boy. One sunny day, in the heart of their neighborhood, Sarah and Ethan were playing at the community park. They wanted to join a game that a group of friends was playing. Sarah gathered her courage, walked up to the group, and said, "Can we play together, please?"

The friends in the group smiled and made room for Sarah and Ethan. They all had a blast playing together, laughing, and cheering each other on. Using "please" was like opening a door to a new friendship adventure!

As the day turned into a beautiful sunset, the children gathered for a snack. Emma was passing out cookies she had baked, and she made sure to say "thank you" to each friend. "Thanks for playing and having fun with us," Emma expressed, spreading gratitude like confetti. The magical words of "thank you" made everyone feel appreciated and happy. It was like a sprinkle of joy over the whole picnic.

As the sun went to sleep and the stars started to twinkle, the children gathered their things to head home. Max realized he had forgotten his ball near the swings. He hurried back, found his ball, and excitedly said, "Excuse me, can I have my ball, please?" A kind lady passing by picked up the ball and handed it to Max with a warm smile. Using "excuse me" was like having a golden ticket to politeness land!

In their cozy homes, the children shared their adventures of the day with their families. They talked about how using kind and polite words made everything more delightful. The parents were proud of their little ones for becoming experts in crafting kind conversations. Imagine kindness is like the most wonderful sprinkle on a cupcake. It makes everything better and more delightful. Being kind means showing love, care, and respect to others and yourself. It's like giving warm hugs with your words and actions.

Let's go on an adventure and explore the amazing world of kindness.

ü Kindness is a Gift: Picture kindness as a present. When you're kind, you give a special gift to someone's heart. It could be a smile, a kind word, or lending a helping hand. Imagine you have a bag of magical kindness gifts to share with the world!

ü Kindness is Contagious: Kindness spreads faster than giggles in a room full of tickles! When you're kind to someone, they feel happy, and they're likely to be kind to others too. It's like starting a chain reaction of happiness and joy. You can be the kindness superstar that makes the world a friendlier place!

ü Kindness Makes Friends: Being kind is like making friendship potions. When you're friendly and caring, you attract friends who appreciate and value you. Kindness is the secret ingredient that bonds friendships and creates beautiful memories.

ü Kindness is a Language: Just like English, Spanish, or any other language, kindness is a universal language. It's like a friendly hello that everyone understands. No matter where you come from or what you believe in, kindness unites us all.

ü Kindness is Brave: It takes courage to be kind, especially when things are tough. Imagine standing up for a friend or helping someone even when you're feeling a little scared. That's bravery in the world of kindness.

ü Kindness to Yourself: Remember, being kind isn't just about others; it's also about treating yourself gently. Imagine you're a cozy, fluffy teddy bear. Being kind to yourself is like giving yourself a warm hug. It's saying, "I'm important, and I deserve love and care too!"

ü Kindness Creates a Happy World: Imagine if everyone sprinkled kindness every day. The world would be a jolly, joyful, and fantastic place! It's like painting a beautiful rainbow of love and compassion everywhere you go.

As you go forward, think of kindness as a treasure, and every act of kindness you make as a shiny jewel to add to your collection. Every smile, every helping hand, and every word spoken with love is like polishing those jewels, making them shine even brighter. Be a kindness superhero in your everyday life. Start by being kind to yourself, and then spread that kindness to others like a wildfire of warmth and care. Your kindness has the power to light up someone's day, to lift them when they're feeling down, and to remind them that they matter.

Remember, in a world where you can be anything, choose to be kind. Let's join hands and create a world where kindness rules, where laughter dances, and where love conquers.

You have the magic within you—now go out and sprinkle kindness everywhere you go!

CHAPTER 8

FRIENDSHIP MAGIC: MAKING REAL FRIENDS

Y ou know a superpower that everyone can have and be the best at the same time? In the world of friendship, being yourself is the most potent enchantment. Real friends appreciate you for who you are, not for pretending to be someone else. It's like having your own unique wand that casts a spell of authenticity. When you show your true colors, you attract people who genuinely like you for you. Embrace your quirks, interests, and personality. Authenticity is the key that unlocks the door to meaningful friendships.

Just like a wizard's wand, kindness has the power to create wonderful connections. Acts of kindness are like magical spells that spread warmth and happiness. Share a smile, offer a helping hand, or say kind words. Small gestures can have a big impact. When you sprinkle kindness, you'll notice how it makes others feel and how it brings you closer to them. That is why I need you to imagine something really cool. Imagine a magical mirror that reflects not your image, but your thoughts and feelings. Listening and understanding others is like using that magical mirror. Everyone wants to be heard and understood. Be a good listener and show empathy towards your friends. Pay attention to what they say and how they feel. Understand their emotions and thoughts and let them know you care.

Just like a magician revealing a magic trick, sharing is a way to build trust and friendship. Share your interests, hobbies, and stories with your friends. Let them into your magical world. When you share a piece of yourself, it deepens your connection with others. Whether it's sharing a toy, a secret, or your time, generosity and sharing create bonds that last.

It is like a magical forest with diverse creatures and plants. Just as the forest thrives on diversity, so do friendships. People are like magical creatures, each with their own unique qualities. Embrace and respect the differences in others. Learn from them and celebrate the diversity that makes the world, and your friendships, magical and enriching.

And don't forget, in every magical tale, there's a hero who stands up against the dark forces. In the world of friendships, you can be that hero. If you see someone being treated unfairly or bullied, stand up for them. Use your voice to spread kindness and defend those in need. Real friends stand up for each other, creating a shield of support and love. Friendship is a beautiful spell that brightens our lives. Remember, making real friends is about being yourself, sprinkling kindness, listening and understanding, sharing your magic, accepting differences, and standing up against bullies. With these friendship secrets, you'll create a magical world of love and friendship around you.

But some things should be remembered before we make friends and embark in this friendship land. In our world of friendship, celebrating each other's successes is a magical act that makes bonds stronger. When a friend accomplishes something special, whether big or small, cheer for them! Celebrate their victories with genuine happiness. Your support and encouragement will amplify their joy and bring you closer.

Patience is another important thing. It is like a wizard's cloak, giving you the power to wait and understand. Friendships take time to grow and develop. Sometimes friends might have challenging moments or different opinions. It's important to be patient and understand each other's feelings. Give space when needed and be there when they're ready to share.

Like a magical artifact, true friendships endure through all kinds of weather. There will be days when things feel tough or confusing. Friends might have disagreements or misunderstandings. Stay true to your friends through the ups and downs. Talk, listen, and find solutions together. A real friend is a constant in the ever-changing magic of life.

But then comes the important question, how do you tell them that you value their friendship? Communication is like a spell book, guiding you through the world of friendships. Be open and honest with your friends. Express your thoughts and feelings clearly and kindly. If something is bothering you, share it respectfully.

Likewise, be a good listener when your friends need to talk. Effective communication helps build trust and understanding, making your friendships even more magical.

And what does that tell them? You become their trusty sidekick. A great guide in the middle of a scary forest. A magical creature that makes them feel better about themselves. Imagine a magical creature that you can always count on. Be that creature for your friends. Be reliable and trustworthy. Keep your promises and be there when your friends need you. Show them they can trust you with their secrets and rely on you in times of joy and sorrow. Trust is the cornerstone of a magical friendship.

In this realm of friendship magic, sharing is the most potent potion. Imagine a cauldron bubbling with the magical essence of togetherness. Sharing isn't just about toys or treats; it's about giving a piece of your heart to your friends. It's the joy of letting others into your magical world, inviting them to be a part of your adventures.

Picture a grand feast where friends gather around a magical table, each bringing their unique dish to share. Sharing laughter, stories, and experiences is like the grand feast of friendship. It creates a sense of unity and belonging, making everyone feel cherished and appreciated. Sharing strengthens the bonds of friendship, turning a simple acquaintance into a cherished companion. But I guess I saved the most important thing for last…

In this grand adventure of friendship, you're the brave wizard exploring the vast magical land. As you journey through the forest of diversity, cross the bridges of kindness, and climb the mountains of loyalty, remember that friendship is a never-ending quest.

Every day brings new opportunities to cast spells of kindness, to listen and understand, to share and celebrate, and to embrace and forgive. Each friendship is a unique story, and you are the author of your own friendship tale. With your heart open and your wand ready, venture forth into the magical realm of friendship, where the possibilities are as endless as the stars in the night sky.

CHAPTER 9

THE POWER OF HONESTY

We all feel like sometimes it is easier to lie in difficult decisions. Like when we spill the juice all over the clean kitchen floor our mom worked so hard to clean in the morning. You don't want to disappoint her; neither do I. So, we blame it on the cat, or on our little brother. But we all also know who it is and putting other people in danger to save ourselves is the same as lying. So it is never a win-win, but always a lose-lose.

Being honest helps build trust between friends. Trust is like a tower made of building blocks. Each time you're honest, you add a block and make the tower stronger. But if you lie, it's like knocking down a block and the tower might fall. Being honest helps friends trust each other more.

Lies can hurt feelings as well. What if your friend told you a story, and you later found out it wasn't true? It might make you sad or confused. Lies can be like little thorns that poke at a friendship. Being honest is like giving a gift of truth to your friends. It helps keep your friendships strong and happy.

Being honest is a good habit, just like brushing your teeth every day. When you're honest often, it becomes a good habit that makes you feel proud. It's a habit that makes your heart happy. Just like how plants grow with water, trust grows with honesty. Because sometimes, a little lie can grow into a big problem, just like a small seed grows into a giant tree. It's easier to stop a little lie when it's small. But if it grows, it can become a big mess. So, it's always better to be honest right from the start.

Honesty isn't always easy, especially when you're worried about disappointing someone. But remember, honesty is like a bright guiding star. It may seem tough at first, but it always leads you to the right path. It's a win-win for your heart and your friendships. Honesty is a shining light that helps you find your way. Even when it's difficult, being honest is the right choice. Let's explore more about honesty and how it can make our friendships stronger and happier.

Sometimes, when we're afraid of getting into trouble, we might tell a small lie. Like, if you accidentally break a plate, you might want to say it wasn't you. But remember, honesty is like a magical cloak that protects you and your friendships. Admitting mistakes takes courage, but it's an important step towards being a trustworthy friend. Have you ever played hide and seek? Lying is like hiding the truth. But when the game is over, you want to find your friends, right? Being honest is like finding your friends after the game. It brings everyone closer and makes the game more fun.

Think of honesty as a seed you plant in a friendship garden. You water it with truth and sunlight, and it grows into a beautiful flower. Lies, on the other hand, are like little bugs that can spoil the garden. Keeping your garden of friendship honest and true makes it a wonderful and joyful place.

Being honest is like being a hero in your own story. Heroes are brave and do what's right, even when it's hard. When you're honest, you become a hero in your friendships. You show others that they can trust you, and that's a powerful magic in friendship. In the grand story of friendship, honesty is the golden thread that weaves everything together. It's what makes the story beautiful, strong, and meaningful. So, let's be brave and embrace the power of honesty in our friendship tale. In the end, honesty always leads to a happy and magical friendship adventure.

The fun part? Honesty ends up becoming an interesting puzzle. Have you ever tried to solve a puzzle without all the pieces? Lies are like missing puzzle pieces. They make it hard to see the whole picture. Honesty, on the other hand, is like finding all the missing pieces and completing the puzzle. It makes everything clear and understandable.

That is not all. It can make you feel big and warm at the same time. Honesty is a bit like being a brave knight. When you're honest, it's like putting on your armor and facing the world with courage. It takes bravery to tell the truth, especially when you've made a mistake. Being honest means being fair too. Imagine you're playing a game, and someone keeps changing the rules. It wouldn't be fair or fun, would it? Honesty is like playing by the rules and making sure everyone has a fair chance to win.

And I am not going to lie to you...Sometimes, telling the truth might feel difficult. It's like being on a high mountain, and honesty is the sturdy rope that helps you climb down safely. It might seem scary, but with honesty as your rope, you can descend safely and face any challenge.

Think of honesty as a strong foundation for a house. A house built on lies would crumble, but a house built on honesty stands tall and firm. It's the basis for trust, understanding, and genuine connections with others. Honesty can be tough in other ways too, especially if you've made a mistake. It's like climbing a steep mountain. But once you reach the top, you feel a sense of accomplishment and freedom. Being honest sets you free from worry and guilt. So I think you can say that honesty is a bit like a strong oak tree. It stands tall and firm, even during a storm. Lies are like the leaves that fall off in the wind, but the tree stays rooted. Honesty keeps us grounded and resilient, no matter what challenges we face.

In the big story of life, honesty is the hero that saves the day. It's the special ingredient that makes everything better. So, let's be brave truth-tellers and let honesty guide us on our incredible life journey. With honesty as our compass, we can navigate through any adventure, knowing that we're on the right path toward a bright and magical future.

CHAPTER 10

TEAM TITANS: UNLEASHING THE POWER OF TOGETHER

Have you ever played a game of soccer or tag with friends? It's more fun when you're part of a team, right? Teamwork is like playing together in a big playground. You pass the ball, share the fun, and cheer each other on. Being a Team Titan means listening to each other's ideas and working towards a common goal. Imagine you're building a sandcastle with friends. Each friend has a role, whether it's digging moats or shaping towers. When you work together, the sandcastle becomes a masterpiece!

Team Titans know that everyone's contribution matters. Just like a puzzle, each piece is unique and important. When you put all the pieces together, you see the bigger picture. Every team member brings something special to create a beautiful, complete picture.

Imagine a relay race, where teammates pass the baton to each other. It's a bit like teamwork—you trust your friends to carry the baton and finish the race. Trust is the glue that holds a team together. When you trust and support each other, you become an unbeatable team. In the grand adventure of life, being a Team Titan is the secret to success and happiness. It's like having a bunch of magical stones, each with a unique power. When you combine these stones, you create a powerful sword.

The best part about being a good, working and supportive team? Being a Team Titan is like having a treehouse with your friends. You all bring different materials and ideas, and together, you build the most amazing treehouse. It's a cozy space where you can all gather, share stories, and have a great time. Teamwork is the strong branches and sturdy trunk that hold your treehouse firmly.

Have you ever watched a group of birds flying together, making intricate patterns in the sky? It's a mesmerizing sight. Just like birds flying in formation, a team works smoothly when everyone knows their role and coordinates with others. Together, you create a beautiful pattern in the sky of life.

And not just birds, NASA thinks so too… Team Titan is a bit like being a team of astronauts in a spaceship. Each astronaut has a role, and they all work together to explore space. Teamwork is the fuel that propels your spaceship through the universe of dreams and achievements. Just like a garden on Earth where each plant has a unique color, shape, and scent. Together, they make the garden a breathtaking paradise. Team Titans are like the diverse plants in the garden of life. When we come together and appreciate each other's uniqueness, we create a beautiful world.

Think of a team as a group of friends setting out on a thrilling treasure hunt. Everyone has a role to play, and when you work together, you find the hidden treasure! Teamwork is like having a treasure map—each friend reads a part of the map, guiding the group to the hidden chest of gold.

Have you ever tried to build the tallest tower of blocks? It's much more exciting when you're building with friends. Teamwork is like stacking blocks together, each friend adding a block to create the tallest tower possible. Together, you achieve things you could never do alone!

It also means being a bit like a family. Imagine you and your friends are like a family baking cookies together. One friend mixes the dough, another shapes the cookies, and someone else puts on the sprinkles. Teamwork is baking those delicious cookies that everyone enjoys, each friend bringing their special ingredients to make them even more tasty!

Team Titans know that everyone's ideas and skills matter. It's like putting together a jigsaw puzzle. Each piece is unique, and when you fit them all together, you reveal a fantastic picture.

Just like being in a rock band. Each member plays a different instrument, but when they play in harmony, they create beautiful music. Teamwork is playing in harmony with your friends, where each person's unique skills come together to make something truly special. Why do you think all superheroes band together in the time of danger?

What do you think about when someone tells you that a new movie about a group of superheroes came out? A team of superheroes, each with a special power. One superhero might have super strength, another can fly, and someone else has the power of invisibility. When they combine their powers, they become a force to be reckoned with! Teamwork is like combining your powers to create the ultimate superhero team.

Have you ever played a game of soccer or tag with friends? It's much more fun and exciting when you're part of a team. Teamwork is like playing a game together, passing the ball, and scoring goals. You cheer for each other and celebrate victories together! Being a Team Titan also means being a bit like a group of brave adventurers exploring a magical forest. Each adventurer has a role to play—someone reads the map, another looks out for danger, and someone else finds the hidden path. Teamwork is like exploring the forest together, combining everyone's knowledge to find the hidden treasure...

Team Titans also know that every member is essential. It's like a group of brave knights protecting a castle. Each knight has their armor and weapon, and when they stand together, they can defend the castle from any threat. Teamwork is like standing together, strong and united, to face challenges head-on.

So let me tell you something that is the most important in this book. Be a chef. No, even better, a group of chefs, a team that knows how to cook the yummiest food ever... Each chef has a special recipe to contribute, and when you combine all the recipes, you create the most delicious feast! Teamwork is like cooking together, each friend adding their special ingredient to make the meal extraordinary.

CHAPTER 11

FEELING DETECTIVES: UNDERSTANDING OUR EMOTIONS

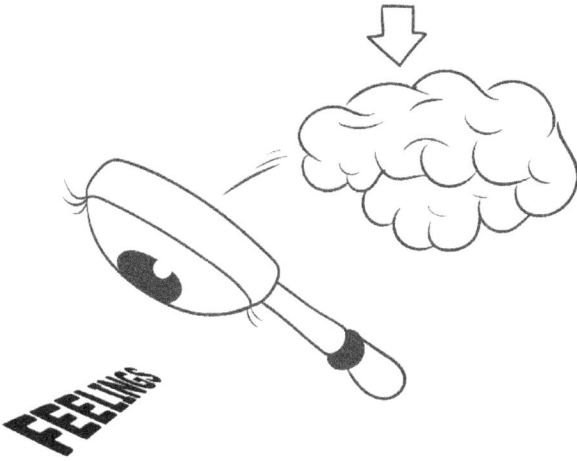

Being a Feeling Detective is like having a special power! It's all about understanding different feelings and learning how to handle them. Are you ready for this exciting adventure to unravel the mysteries of our emotions?

In life, we experience a wide range of emotions. Sometimes we're as joyful as a playful puppy, and other times we might feel a bit down, like a rainy day. It's perfectly normal to feel all sorts of emotions! Each emotion is like a piece of a colorful puzzle that makes us unique and special. Just like detectives solve mysteries, we can solve the mysteries of our feelings! Picture yourself putting on your detective hat and grabbing your magnifying glass. As Feeling Detectives, we ask ourselves questions to uncover the clues about how we're feeling. Are we excited, worried, happy, or maybe a mix of everything? The more we understand, the better we can help ourselves and our friends.

Let's open our "Emotion Toolbox" and see what tools we have to help us on this adventure:

Talking about it: Sharing our feelings with a trusted friend or family member can make us feel lighter and happier. It's like having a sidekick on our emotion-solving mission!

Taking deep breaths: When our feelings feel too big, taking deep breaths is our superpower. Inhale courage, exhale worries! It helps us feel calmer and ready to tackle anything.

Drawing or writing: Expressing our feelings through art or words is like creating a treasure map of our emotions. It helps us understand and solve the mystery within us.

Doing something we love: Sometimes, doing things we enjoy, like playing our favorite games or spending time in nature, can chase away the grumpy clouds and bring back the sunshine!

And guess what? We're not on this adventure alone! We're a team of Feeling Detectives, ready to support each other. Sometimes a friend might need our help, just like we might need theirs. We're like a super team of caring hearts, always looking out for one another. Life is like an incredible rollercoaster ride of feelings! It's okay to enjoy the highs and handle the lows. As Feeling Detectives, we're always learning and growing, discovering the magical world of emotions.

Imagine our emotions as colorful planets in the galaxy of our hearts and minds. Each planet has its own unique atmosphere and landscape, just like each emotion has its own feeling and story. Our job as Feeling Detectives is to explore these planets and understand them better.

Let's blast off to Planet Joy! This planet is all about happiness and excitement. It's like a land of rainbows, where laughter and smiles light up the sky. When we're on Planet Joy, everything feels like an awesome adventure, and we want to share our joy with everyone around us!

Next, we'll journey to Planet Worry. This planet might have some clouds and storms, but that's okay! It's natural to feel worried or anxious sometimes. Being a Feeling Detective means visiting this planet and figuring out what's causing the worry. Together, we can calm the storms and find sunshine again. Our spaceship then takes us to Planet Sadness. It might seem a little gloomy here, but every Feeling Detective knows that sadness is a part of the emotional galaxy. It's like the rain that helps plants grow. We can visit this planet, understand why we're feeling sad, and help the sunshine through the clouds.

But now what? We have to make a quick stop at Planet Anger. This planet has some fiery volcanoes, but it's important to remember that anger, like volcanoes, can cool down with time and understanding. We can explore this planet, understand our anger, and find healthy ways to express it.

Now right at the end when you thought the spaceship was about to land back at home, we'll fly over to Planet Love and Kindness. This is a peaceful planet where love, care, and kindness bloom like beautiful flowers. Being a Feeling Detective means spreading love and kindness everywhere we go, making the galaxy a better place.

Back on our home planet, Earth, we know that being a Feeling Detective is an incredible adventure. Every feeling we have is like a star in the vast sky, lighting up our lives in different ways. Emotions make our journey exciting and colorful. Being a Feeling Detective is about understanding our feelings, just like understanding different colors. You know how you feel happy when you play with your favorite toy or see a rainbow? That's like feeling joyful! Joyful is when your heart feels super excited and full of happiness.

Sometimes, you might worry about something, like a big test coming up. Feeling worried is like having lots of questions in your mind. It's okay to be worried; everyone feels that way sometimes. What helps is talking to someone you trust, like a parent or teacher. They can help you find answers and make the worry go away.

Feeling sad is when you have a frown on your face and might want to be alone for a bit. Maybe you feel sad when you miss a friend or can't find your favorite toy. Feeling sad is like having a little rain cloud over your head. But just like the rain goes away, so do sad feelings. You can talk to someone you trust, and they can help bring the sunshine back… so no worries.

Have you ever been so mad that you wanted to stomp your feet or yell? That's feeling angry! Feeling angry is like having a fire inside you that needs to cool down. It's okay to feel angry, but it's important to express it in a healthy way. You can take deep breaths, count to ten, or even talk about why you're upset.

Being a Feeling Detective means understanding and embracing these emotions. Each feeling is like a different color in a beautiful painting, and when you mix them, you get a fantastic picture of you! It's important to know that everyone has these feelings, and it's okay to talk about them. We're all on this feeling adventure together!

CHAPTER 12

ZEN GARDEN OF THE MIND: SECRETS OF INNER PEACE

Welcome to the Peaceful Mind garden, a quiet place inside us where we learn how to be really calm and peaceful. Just like a garden with beautiful flowers and gentle breezes, our minds can also be peaceful and calm. In our busy world, finding a moment to be calm is like finding a hidden treasure. Imagine a small lake that's so still, it reflects the sky like a mirror. That stillness is like the peace we want inside us. We can find it by taking a few quiet moments each day to sit down, close our eyes, and take slow, deep breaths. It's like letting the little waves settle, creating a sense of calm inside us.

In the middle of a busy day, we can sit down, close our eyes, and take a few deep breaths. Breathing in and out, slowly and calmly, helps us feel relaxed. It's like pressing a pause button in our minds.

When our minds are calm, it's easier to think clearly. Imagine your thoughts are like colorful fish swimming in a pond. With a calm mind, we can see the fish clearly and understand our thoughts better. Sometimes, thoughts can be like butterflies, fluttering around and making us feel restless. The peaceful mind helps us catch those butterflies, gently and one by one. We can let go of the busy thoughts and just focus on being here, right now.

Have you ever watched leaves gently falling from trees? That's how we can let go of thoughts that bother us. We acknowledge them and then imagine them gently floating away like falling leaves. It's a way of saying, "It's okay, thought. I'll let you go for now." In our peaceful garden, we can also water the flowers of kindness and gratitude. Just like taking care of a garden, taking care of our thoughts and being kind to ourselves and others makes our minds even more peaceful.

Inner peace is like having a cozy, quiet space inside us. It's a place where we can go whenever we feel a bit lost or upset. We close our eyes, take a few deep breaths, and imagine ourselves in this peaceful garden. It's a garden of our own making, where we're always welcome. In this peaceful garden of the mind, we can also imagine our worries as little pebbles. We gather them, one by one, and gently place them by the side of a clear, flowing stream. As we let go of our worries, it's like the stream carries them away, leaving us feeling lighter.

Does a cozy blanket make you feel safe and warm? Our peaceful mind is like that cozy blanket. It wraps us in a sense of safety and comfort, no matter what's happening around us. When we're in our peaceful garden, we can think of happy memories or beautiful places we've been to. It's like flipping through a picture book filled with joyful moments. Remembering these moments can bring a smile to our faces and make our peaceful garden even more wonderful.

Being in our peaceful mind garden also helps us be kind to ourselves. We're all growing, just like flowers in a garden. Sometimes we might make mistakes, and that's okay. Our peaceful mind reminds us to be gentle with ourselves, just like we would be gentle with a tender plant. As we continue to visit our peaceful garden, we might discover new things about ourselves. Maybe we have a favorite spot in our garden—a special place that makes us feel especially calm and happy. We can visit that spot often, even in our imagination, whenever we need a moment of peace.

In the grand adventure of life, our peaceful mind is like a secret superpower. It helps us stay strong, kind, and focused. With our peaceful minds, we can face challenges and celebrate the good times, knowing that we always have this special, peaceful place within us.

We can also practice gratitude. Gratitude is like planting seeds of happiness in the soil of our minds. We can think about the good things in our lives, like the love of our family, the fun we have with friends or even the tasty food we get to eat. Each thought of gratitude is like watering those seeds, helping them grow into beautiful flowers of happiness.

Just like a garden needs a little tender loving care, our minds need love too. We can be kind to ourselves by saying positive and encouraging words in our minds. It's like giving our minds a warm hug. "I am kind, I am brave, and I am loved," are words that can make our minds feel safe and cared for.

It is also a wonderful time to dream. We can dream about all the amazing things we want to do and be. Dreams are like the colorful butterflies that visit our garden. We can watch them, chase them, and let them inspire us to reach for the stars. Our peaceful garden is always there for us, even on tough days. When we're feeling sad, upset, or scared, we can close our eyes, take a deep breath, and imagine ourselves in our garden. It's a peaceful oasis that we carry with us wherever we go.

And guess what? We can share the magic of our peaceful garden with others too. We can tell our friends about it and imagine them in their peaceful gardens. We can spread peace and happiness, making the world a more peaceful and beautiful place for everyone.

In the story of our lives, our peaceful mind is like the heart of the tale. It's where our hopes, dreams, and love reside. So, let's keep tending to our peaceful garden, nurturing it with kindness, gratitude, and dreams, making it a truly magical and peaceful place to be.

CHAPTER 13

THE PEACEFUL PLACE: CALM ADVENTURE

Imagine a day with no rushing, no hurrying. That's what being in our peaceful place feels like. It's like finding a cozy, soft pillow where we can rest our minds. We can close our eyes and take a slow, deep breath, letting the worries float away, just like leaves gently falling from trees. In our peaceful place, there's a beautiful garden. The air is filled with the sweet scent of flowers, and colorful butterflies dance around. This garden is our very own, and we can make it just the way we like it. We can plant our favorite flowers of happy thoughts and gratitude. Watching them bloom is like feeling our heart bloom with joy.

Imagine a soft, comfy chair in our peaceful place. We can sit there and read a book, imagine exciting adventures, or just listen to the sound of birds singing. It's a special place where we feel safe, loved, and at peace.

In this peaceful adventure, we can also listen to our favorite calming music. It's like a gentle lullaby for our minds, helping us drift into a land of quiet and tranquility. It's amazing how music can take us to places of calmness and make our hearts feel lighter. Sometimes, we might find little pebbles of worries or fears in our peaceful place. That's okay. We can pick them up, examine them, and then toss them gently into a stream. Watching the pebbles float away is like watching our worries disappear.

Our peaceful place is a treasure chest of calmness. We can visit it whenever we need a break from the busy world. It's like having a superpower that helps us face challenges and feel stronger inside. Learning to be calm is like having a magical key that unlocks many doors in the grand adventure of life. As kids, we're always discovering new things and facing different situations. Sometimes, things might not go the way we want them to. Maybe we can't solve a puzzle, or a friend doesn't want to play. That's when our magical calmness key becomes incredibly useful.

When we're calm, our minds work like a wise wizard. We can think clearly and make better decisions. Imagine being in a race. If we rush and panic, we might trip and fall. But if we stay calm, we can run steadily and reach the finish line smoothly. Being calm is also like having a shield that protects us from feeling too upset or angry. Maybe someone accidentally bumps into us. Instead of getting mad, we can take a deep breath and calmly say, "It's okay." That way, we spread a little calmness to others too.

In school, being calm is a secret to doing well. If we have a big test or a challenging assignment, being calm helps us focus and do our best. It's like having a magic wand that helps us stay on track and learn new things.

And here's a really important part: being calm helps us in our friendships too. Sometimes, our friends might feel upset, and if we stay calm and listen, we can be like a comforting blanket for them. Our calmness can help them feel better, just like a warm hug.

As we grow up, being calm becomes even more crucial. When we face big challenges, like choosing what we want to be when we grow up, being calm helps us think clearly and make important decisions. It's like having a treasure map that leads us to our dreams and goals.

It is like having a secret potion that helps us during tricky moments. Imagine you're playing a game, and it gets a bit hard. If you get frustrated and upset, the game becomes less fun. But if you take a deep breath, stay calm, and try again, the game becomes an exciting adventure!

As we grow, we'll have bigger adventures like facing tests, making new friends, or trying new activities. Being calm during these adventures is like having a trusty map. It helps us find our way through challenges and keeps us from feeling lost.

Imagine being on a swing. When we push the swing gently, it goes back and forth smoothly. But if we push too hard, it might stop or swing erratically. Our minds are a bit like that swing. When we're calm, our thoughts swing smoothly, and we can enjoy the ride of our day. Another amazing thing about being calm is that it's contagious... What does that mean? It can spread so fast and so happily. It is not a disease so no worries at all. It is the opposite. The best thing to happen ever. If you're calm, it can help others around you stay calm too. Your calmness can be like a cozy blanket that wraps around your friends, making everyone feel safe and peaceful.

So, let's practice being calm, just like practicing a new game or learning to ride a bike. Each time we practice, it becomes easier and more natural. And soon, being calm will be like second nature, making our lives more enjoyable and our adventures more exciting!

CHAPTER 14

BOUNCE BACK HEROES: GETTING STRONG AGAIN

Today, we're diving into the world of "Bounce Back Heroes," where we learn the incredible art of bouncing back and becoming strong when things don't go the way we planned. Imagine you're playing with a bouncy ball. When you bounce it, it might not always go in the direction you wanted. That's okay! Bouncing back means being able to smile, pick up the ball, and bounce it again. Life is a lot like that—sometimes things don't go as planned, and that's when our bouncing-back skills come in handy!

This will also require a short little break. Like a big breath too. Just to calm down, remember? Taking a deep breath is like pressing a reset button. When something doesn't go as we hoped, we can pause, take a deep breath, and gather our strength. It's like getting ready for the next bounce! Deep breaths help us calm down and think clearly about what to do next.

Being positive is like wearing a superhero cape. It gives us the courage to face challenges. If we spill some milk, instead of frowning, we can say, "Oops! Let's clean it up and try again." Positivity helps us find solutions and keeps our spirits high, just like a bouncy ball that always springs back up. Like trying to build a tower with blocks, and it keeps falling. Instead of feeling down, we can learn from each fall. Maybe we need to place the blocks differently or try a new strategy. Learning from our "oops" moments make us even better Bounce Back Heroes!

We're all in this bouncing adventure together. When we share our bounce-back stories with friends, we help them be Bounce Back Heroes too. Maybe your story will inspire a friend to bounce back from their own little bumps in the road.

In life's big storybook, being a Bounce Back Hero is a remarkable chapter. It's about facing challenges with a smile, standing tall even when things are tough, and remembering that every fall is a chance to bounce back stronger. Imagine this: You're the captain of the Bounce Back Squad, leading your team through the ups and downs of the epic Adventureland. Sometimes, you hit a speed bump, and it's like, "Whoa, unexpected twist!" But no worries, you're the expert at bouncing back and turning those twists into twirls of triumph.

Every adventure needs a power-up, right? Deep breaths are your power-up potions. When things get as tangled as spaghetti, take a deep breath, and untangle the mess. Suddenly, you're ready to face the world, armed with spaghetti-slinging confidence. And remember, positivity is your magical wand. Wave it, and "abracadabra," everything's more colorful and exciting! When life decides to play a prank, just smile and say, "Nice one, life! But watch me turn this into a comedy show!"

Remember that tower of blocks? Sometimes, it's like life decides to give it a little nudge, and down it goes! But that's when you, the Master Builder of Bouncing Back, gather those blocks and build an even cooler tower.

Sharing your bounce-back tales is like a victory dance. You show others the moves to rock this dance floor called life. You say, "Hey, I slipped on a banana peel once, but look at me now, doing the moonwalk of success!"

Oops moments are just plot twists in our story. It's like being the director of your own movie, and sometimes you yell, "Cut!" Mistakes are the funny behind-the-scenes bloopers that make our adventure even more entertaining. Embrace those oops moments, for they're the spices in the recipe of life.

Sharing bounce-back tales is like having your own fan club. You're the rockstar, and everyone's cheering for you! When you share your stories, you inspire others to rock their own show. It's a grand concert of bouncing back, and we're all headlining. In the spectacular saga of life, being a Bounce Back Hero is having the coolest superpower. You're the hero of your story, facing challenges, acing the levels, and unlocking secret achievements. Keep being the superhero you are because you're totally rocking this adventure!

So, tune up your air guitar, put on your funky shades, and let's keep jamming through this adventure called life! But, my question to you, brave reader, is do you want to be great at this... stare life in its eyes and win? You have to become a maestro for that. A maestro is someone who is so good at something they help others learn it and become great themselves.

A Bounce Back Maestro is like being a captain of a ship. Sometimes, the sea of life gets a little stormy, and your ship rocks and sways. But guess what? You're the captain, and you've got the skills to navigate through any storm. You steer that ship with courage and a big ol' smile, singing sea shanties all the way.

Being a Bounce Back Maestro means you're an amazing painter. Life gives you a canvas, and sometimes it spills a few buckets of paint on it. You take a step back, and think, "What can I make with these splashes?" And voilà! You turn those accidental splatters into a beautiful, colorful masterpiece.

Oops moments? They're like plot twists in the grand storybook of life. Imagine you're reading an adventure book, and suddenly the story takes an unexpected turn. You giggle, turn the page, and eagerly read on. Life's oops moments are those exciting, unexpected turns that make our story worth reading and sharing.

CHAPTER 15

PUZZLE-SOLVING MASTERS: TURNING PROBLEMS INTO TREASURES

Today, we're setting sail on the exciting seas of "Puzzle-Solving Masters," where we uncover the hidden treasures of turning problems into exciting adventures. I just need you to use the brilliant skill of imagination and think of life as a grand treasure hunt. Sometimes, you stumble upon a tricky puzzle. It might make you scratch your head and say, "Hmm," but guess what? You've got a map, a compass, and a heart full of courage to solve that puzzle and discover the treasure!

Picture puzzles as secret doorways in the walls of a castle. Each puzzle is like a unique key that unlocks a hidden chamber of knowledge and growth. When you face a puzzle, it's an invitation to an adventure, a chance to put on your thinking cap and embark on a quest. Being a Puzzle-Solving Master means having a toolbox filled with awesome tools. Tools like curiosity, creativity, and a pinch of persistence. With these tools in hand, no puzzle is too daunting; no challenge is too difficult. You can fix the leaks in your ship and sail smoothly through the storm…

The "oops" moments in this adventure are like finding a puzzle piece you thought you lost. Sometimes, things don't go as planned, but those unexpected twists are what make the puzzle interesting. Every "oops" is a hint, a clue that helps you solve the puzzle of life with a triumphant smile!

When you solve a puzzle, it's like finding a golden treasure chest. But the real magic is in sharing your treasure with your fellow adventurers. Share your puzzle-solving tales, your strategies, and the joy of victory. Together, we create a treasure map for others to navigate their own puzzles!

In the epic tale of life, being a Puzzle-Solving Master is having a magical wand. With a flick and a swish, you transform problems into opportunities, obstacles into steppingstones, and challenges into triumphs. Now that we've set the stage for our adventure, let's delve deeper into the skills and qualities that make a true Puzzle-Solving Master. Each of these qualities is like a gleaming gem that adds brilliance to your treasure-hunting quest.

Curiosity: The Shining Beacon

Imagine curiosity as a shining beacon, lighting your way through the darkest corners of the puzzle. It's the spark that ignites your quest for knowledge and discovery. Never be afraid to ask questions, explore the unknown, and seek out new possibilities. Curiosity opens doors and reveals hidden pathways, guiding you toward the treasure.

Creativity: The Magic Paintbrush

Creativity is your magic paintbrush, allowing you to color the world with your imagination and vision. When faced with a puzzle, think outside the box. Let your creativity flow and paint vibrant solutions. Sometimes, the most unexpected strokes of creativity lead to the most breathtaking masterpieces.

Persistence: The Unyielding Shield

Picture persistence as an unyielding shield, guarding you against discouragement and setbacks. Challenges may arise, but with persistence, you stand strong and keep forging ahead. Every attempt, no matter how small, is a step closer to unraveling the puzzle and claiming the treasure.

Teamwork: The Strength of Unity

In this grand adventure, you're never alone. Teamwork is the strength of unity, a force that multiplies your abilities and propels you forward. Collaborate with your fellow adventurers, share your insights, and learn from one another. Together, you can conquer even the most perplexing puzzles.

Resilience: The Invincible Armor

Resilience is your invincible armor, shielding you from disappointment and doubt. When faced with failures or unexpected twists, bounce back stronger. Learn from your experiences and use them to fortify your resolve. Remember, setbacks are just detours on the road to success.

Now, dear adventurers, as we embark on this puzzle-solving journey, keep these gems close to your heart. Let curiosity light your way, creativity guide your hand, persistence fuel your spirit, teamwork empower you, and resilience armor you against any challenges you may face. When you face a problem, think of it like the coolest puzzle ever... Look at it in different ways, like turning it around to see all sides of it. Problems are like exciting challenges waiting for you to solve, not scary things you can't beat. Mistakes you make are like hints on a treasure map—they help you figure out how to do better next time!

Being able to change and try new things is super important. It's like being able to switch your toys while playing a game. Sometimes you need to change your plans a little to make things work better, just like adjusting your moves in a game.

It's also awesome to cheer for yourself! Even small progress is like taking a step closer to winning a game. Remember to be thankful for the good stuff too—it's like saying "thank you" for winning a prize. Picture yourself beating the problem, like pretending you're a superhero saving the day. It helps you believe you can do it. Think of this adventure as a super fun treasure hunt! Each problem you solve is like finding a new hidden treasure. Keep going, and you'll become a super-duper Puzzle-Solving Master, finding all the cool secrets in the world, one puzzle at a time!

CHAPTER 16

THE POWER OF "THANK YOU": APPRECIATING AND EXPRESSING GRATITUDE

Welcome to a special chapter all about saying "Thank You" and how it can make the world a better place. "Thank You" is like a magical word that fills hearts with happiness and spreads smiles everywhere.

Imagine "Thank You" as a sprinkle of fairy dust. When you say it, you spread happiness to others, just like fairy dust spreads magic. Let's learn why saying "Thank You" is super important and how we can use this magic to make our world sparkle with kindness!

A simple "Thank You" can change people's days and make them feel better about themselves. Who doesn't want that? Saying "Thank You" shows appreciation for what others do for us. It's like giving them a big hug of gratitude. When people feel appreciated, it makes them happy and encourages them to keep being awesome!

"Thank You" is also a small act of kindness that creates a ripple effect. When someone is kind to you, saying "Thank You" is like passing on that kindness. It's like sharing a warm cookie with a friend!

Imagine "Thank You" as a friendship glue. When we express our gratitude, it strengthens our friendships and makes our bonds with others even more awesome. But how can you find great ways to say thank you?

Lucky for you, I have you covered…

1. **Say it Loud and Proud:** Simply saying "Thank You" with a smile brightens someone's day. It's like a sunbeam of happiness.

2. **Write a Thank You Note:** Drawing a picture or writing a note saying "Thank You" is like sending a hug on paper. It's a sweet surprise that makes people feel special.

3. **Give a Thank You Hug**: Hugs are super warm and fuzzy. Giving someone a hug to say "Thank You" is like giving them a big, cozy blanket of gratitude.

4. **Make a Thank You Card**: Get creative and make a card! Add colors, stickers, and your favorite drawings. It's a fun way to say, "Thank You" and show your artistic side!

5. **Bake or Cook a Thank You Treat:** If you like baking or cooking, making a special treat is a delicious way to say, "Thank You." Sharing goodies is like spreading extra smiles.

Friends love to hear "Thank You" because it shows that you appreciate and care about them. Just like a puzzle coming together perfectly, "Thank You" helps our friendships fit and connect in the best way possible...

But saying "Thank You" isn't just about making others feel good; it's about making you feel good too! When you express gratitude, it's like a sprinkle of happiness on your own heart. It reminds you of all the wonderful things and people you have in your life. It's like a gratitude hug for yourself!

And guess what? You can say "Thank You" not only to people but also to nature, the world around you, and even to yourself. Thank the sun for shining, the rain for helping plants grow, and thank yourself for being awesome! The more "Thank You" we sprinkle, the more we fill the world with love and positivity.

Let's also remember to be thankful for the challenges and lessons life gives us. Even when things are tough, they help us grow and become stronger, just like how rain helps flowers grow. So, thank you, challenges, for making us the amazing people we are. Now, it's your turn to spread the "Thank You" magic! Who can you thank today? It could be a friend, a family member, a teacher, or even a friendly neighbor. Maybe you could thank the mail carrier for bringing letters or thank a tree for providing shade. Let's make it a "Thank You" adventure—how many smiles can you create with your magic words of gratitude today?

CHAPTER 17

LAUGHTER MAGIC: FINDING JOY IN HUMOR AND PLAY

Are you ready to become a laughter wizard, spreading joy and giggles wherever you go? Let's make laughter a part of our daily magical adventures. Remember, a hearty laugh is like a potion of happiness, and you're the alchemist brewing it.

Laughter is a universal language that transcends barriers and connects us all. It's a magical force that can turn any frown upside down and fill our hearts with warmth and happiness. The sound of laughter is like music to our souls, and the contagious nature of laughter means that when one person starts to laugh, it's not long before others join in, creating a beautiful symphony of joy.

The magic of laughter lies in its ability to bring happiness. When we laugh, it's as if we're stirring a cauldron of joy, creating a potion that bubbles with positive energy. Laughter is infectious, spreading from one person to another like wildfire. It's the kind of infectiousness we all welcome and cherish. Imagine being a wizard or a witch, conjuring laughter spells that make everyone around you feel a little lighter and happier.

And what about something that uplifts a bad mood? Laughter is a healer too. It has the power to mend wounds, soothe aches, and lift spirits. During tough times, a good laugh can act as a soothing balm for the soul. It's a reminder that even in the darkest of moments, there's light and joy to be found. Laughter is a lifeline, a magical rope that pulls us out of the depths of sadness and allows us to breathe in the fresh air of happiness.

Have you ever noticed how laughing more brings people closer? It's like a bonding spell that creates a sense of togetherness. When we share laughter with others, it's like we're saying, "We're in this magical adventure of life together!" Laughter knits friendships tightly, making them resilient and joyful. It's the glue that keeps us connected, and the memories of shared laughter are like cherished treasures in the vault of our hearts.

Laughter is also something we can use to level ourselves with each other, you know, becoming true to yourself. It doesn't matter who you are, where you come from, or what language you speak—laughter is a language everyone understands. It unites us in a way that few other things can. In the realm of laughter, we're all equals, sharing the delightful experience of mirth and amusement.

So let's get on to discovering some fun ways to find laughter magic in our everyday lives. Silly jokes are like ticklish spells for your funny bone. They make you giggle and laugh, spreading happiness wherever you go. Create your own jokes and share them with friends for an extra dose of laughter. Picture yourself as a wizard of jokes, casting spells of laughter that make everyone chuckle and smile.

Watching funny shows or cartoons is another delightful way to tap into the magic of laughter. These shows are like laughter potions in a magic cauldron. They have the power to make you laugh out loud and create a world of giggles. Imagine you're on a laughter adventure, exploring a land where every corner is filled with humor and joy.

Playing games that involve silliness and laughter is like a laughter potion explosion! Try games where you make funny faces, imitate animals, or tell hilarious stories. Let the laughter rain down like confetti, creating a playful atmosphere of joy and amusement. In this magical realm of games, you're the laughter wizard, casting spells that make everyone laugh and grin from ear to ear.

Ever had a silly dance party? It's one of the most delightful ways to infuse your day with laughter and joy. Put on your favorite tunes and have a dance party where you can dance in the silliest way possible! Dance like a robot, a wiggly worm, or a spinning top. Let the laughter dance with you, and imagine that your dance moves are spells, spreading happiness to everyone around you.

And let's not forget the magic of sharing silly stories. Create and share silly and imaginative stories with your friends or family. Each person adds a sentence to the story, and you'll end up with a magical, laughter-filled tale. It's like being part of a wizarding storytelling circle, where each word you add weaves a magical thread of laughter.

Just imagine a world where everyone had a laughter potion — a little vial of laughter they could sip from whenever they felt down.

Laughter has the power to transform our perspective and turn a gloomy day into a day filled with sunshine and rainbows. It's like a wizard's spell that can change the color of the sky, making it a vibrant and joyful blue.

Have you ever noticed how laughter gives you a burst of energy, like a magical power-up? It's like you've found a secret stash of energy potions that instantly rejuvenates you. Laughter charges you up, making you ready to take on the magical quests of the day.

Remember, you're a laughter wizard, and your laughter is your magic spell. Use it to spread joy, brighten someone's day, and create a world where laughter echoes in every corner. Just as a wizard hones their magical skills, keep practicing your laughter spells, and soon you'll be a laughter wizard extraordinaire!

Now, it's your turn to spread the laughter magic! Who can you share a laugh with today? It could be a friend, a sibling, a teacher, or even your pet. Maybe you could tell a funny joke to your family during dinner or have a silly dance party with your friends. Let's make it a laughter adventure—how many smiles can you create with your magic of mirth today?

CHAPTER 18

CHANGE CHAMPION GUIDE: GETTING READY FOR NEW ADVENTURES

Buckle up, we're strapping on our adventure helmets and revving up for a rollercoaster of exciting changes. Think of it as stepping onto a brand-new amusement park ride, where every twist and turn brings a thrill and a cheer.

Imagine you're the captain of a magical spaceship, zooming through the universe of changes. These changes are like colorful planets, each with its own surprises and fun. Sometimes, change is like discovering a new flavor of ice cream — exciting and delicious. But we need to know about this cool thing called a "Change Champion Guide." Picture it as your trusty treasure map for exploring the lands of change. Just like a pirate captain reading a map to find hidden treasures, you'll use your "Change Champion Guide" to find exciting adventures.

As we set sail, the first island on our map is "Learning New Things." Learning is like unlocking secret levels in a video game. Each new thing you learn is a key that opens a door to an amazing adventure. Whether it's learning to ride a bike or discovering a new planet in your favorite book, learning is always an exciting quest.

Next up, we've got "Making New Friends." Making friends is like finding a special type of star in the vast galaxy of people. Each friend you make adds sparkle to your journey, lighting up your path and making the adventure even more fantastic. Let's zoom into the "Trying New Hobbies" zone. Trying new hobbies is like wearing a disguise and becoming a space detective on a mission. It's all about discovering what makes your heart dance with joy. Whether it's painting, playing a musical instrument, or playing a new sport, every hobby is a new adventure waiting to unfold.

But what's an adventure without a bit of "Facing Fears"? Facing fears is like having a magical shield that makes you braver and stronger. It's about conquering the dragons of worry and discovering your superhero powers. Remember, bravery turns every fear into an exciting challenge waiting to be won! So, you know what? We'll dock at the "Dreaming Big" island. Dreaming big is like being the hero in your own story, with a grand quest to fulfill. Your dreams are like shooting stars, and every time you wish upon one, you get a step closer to making your adventure dreams come true.

Just like when you pack your backpack before a big journey, life also has moments when we need to prepare for new experiences. It is like being an adventurer about to go on a new journey. Before you set off, you need to collect your supplies and make a plan. Life is a lot like that—full of exciting adventures waiting for you. But to make the most of them, it's important to be prepared.

Getting ready for new adventures means being open to change. Change is like a new chapter in your favorite storybook—it brings surprises, challenges, and learning new things. Just as you eagerly turn the pages to discover what happens next, life invites us to accept change with curiosity and enthusiasm.

Change can be as simple as starting a new school year, moving to a new home, or trying a different hobby. These changes can make you feel excited, but they might also make you a bit nervous. That's perfectly okay! We understand that it's okay to feel a mix of emotions when something new is happening around you.

One way to prepare for change is by setting goals. Goals are like treasure maps that guide you toward your dreams. They help you focus on what you want to achieve and make the journey more exciting. For example, if you're starting a new school year, your goal might be to make new friends or learn something new every day. Planning is another superhero tool in your toolkit. Just like a builder creates a blueprint before constructing a house, planning helps you map out your path to success. It's like drawing a map for your adventure, marking all the exciting stops along the way.

As a young adventurer, you also know the power of a positive attitude. A positive attitude is like a sunny day—it brightens your journey and makes challenges easier to overcome. When you face change with optimism and a smile, you're ready to turn even the rainiest day into an adventure.

Young adventurers can become true champions by understanding that they're not alone on their journeys. Just like you have friends and family to support you, there are always people who want to help when you're facing change. Don't be afraid to ask for help or talk about your feelings. Sharing your thoughts and concerns is like having a team of cheerleaders by your side, rooting for your success.

But going on a new exploration also needs a new backpack that has all the things you need. This can include a lot of things. Your adventure backpack is like a magic kit, filled with tools to help you on your journey. First, you'll want a sturdy pair of curiosity goggles to help you see and understand new things. These goggles are like windows into the unknown, allowing you to observe and learn.

Next, toss in a handful of courage pebbles. Whenever you're a little nervous about trying something new, you can hold a pebble and remind yourself that you've got the courage to face any challenge that comes your way. Don't forget the imagination map! It's a special treasure that helps you dream big and plan your adventures. You can unfold it whenever you need a boost of creativity or want to set exciting goals.

A snack of positivity is a must. Fill a small container with positive thoughts and happy memories. When things get tough, take a bite of your snack, and it'll give you the energy to keep going. And don't forget to pack a compass of kindness to help you navigate through new friendships and experiences. Kindness is like a magnet — it attracts good things and good people to your journey.

Include a blanket of laughter for moments when you need a bit of fun and joy. It's like a cozy hug that reminds you to enjoy the adventure and smile along the way.

And you are set!

CHAPTER 19

THE NATURE EXPEDITION: LEARNING FROM MOTHER EARTH

Being curious is the best part of this world. When you are young and full of energy, you can use your time to look for answers and come up with many great ideas to explore new things. Everything is a mystery that needs a smart detective like you. Now, you may ask me, what can I look for as a mystery that I can learn and enjoy? You don't have to look around too far. It is the grass under your feet, the sky above you that is so blue and bright as your smile on a good day, and that can also be as gray as the road and start to cry whenever it is having a hard day. It is only the sky after all. What about the trees? Every tree that you see when you walk for more than five minutes to anywhere, is so different. The leaves differ in size, shape, and color. That reminds me of the flowers. Yellow, pink, red, purple, and sometimes even white. Do you know there are black flowers too? So many types of black flowers. Isn't that fascinating?

Think of it like being a little scientist, learning fascinating secrets from Mother Earth. Picture yourself as a brave Nature Detective, ready to solve the mysteries of the natural world. Nature is like a magical garden, filled with all sorts of incredible plants and animals. Imagine you're a gardener in this magical garden, taking care of the flowers, trees, and bushes. Just as a gardener nurtures the plants they love, we can nurture our knowledge and curiosity about nature.

The world becomes a big library, but this one is filled with books about the great outdoors. Each book has a different story — stories about plants growing, animals playing, and rivers flowing. Exploring these books is like going on an expedition, discovering new chapters of Mother Earth's incredible tale. That is not it… Learning from Mother Earth is like having a wonderful teacher. She teaches us about balance and harmony. Just like the sun and the moon take turns in the sky, we learn about finding balance in our lives. It's like dancing to the rhythm of nature, swaying with the wind, and flowing with the rivers.

Mother Earth also teaches us about patience. Just like a seed turns into a beautiful flower with time, we too grow and learn gradually. It's like watching a butterfly emerge from a cocoon — a slow and beautiful transformation. As Nature Detectives, we can learn about working as a team by watching animals work together. It's like being in a team with your friends, each one playing an important role to achieve a goal. Just like ants carrying food to their home, we too can accomplish great things when we cooperate and help each other.

You become the painter, and the colors on your palette are the elements of nature — earth, water, air, and sunlight. These elements come together to create a beautiful painting of our planet. By learning about these elements, we know about harmony and balance in our own lives. Harmony is how we live together with so many different kinds of animals, beautiful plants, and other people like us, in a way that all of us are happy and helpful to each other. If we do not act in harmony, some animals, plants, or people can become hurt and lose things that are important to them.

Discovering nature is like an endless storybook full of excitement! Picture each tree, flower, and tiny bug as a page in this book of adventures. As we explore the pages of nature, we uncover amazing tales. Some stories are about plants growing, starting as tiny seeds, and turning into tall trees that give homes and shade to birds. Other stories show busy bees collecting nectar from flowers, helping plants make new seeds. Nature is like a super cool library filled with stories of growing, working together, and looking beautiful.

Let's be curious nature explorers, ready with our special glasses and notebooks, just like detectives! We watch and gather clues from the world around us. Every bug, leaf, and cloud has its own story. The more we listen, the more we learn the awesome secrets of nature. Did you know that plants use sunlight to make their own food, a bit like how you eat your favorite snacks to get energy?

That's a super cool nature fact, and there are many more waiting for us to find…

Mother Earth is like the best teacher, and the outdoors is our classroom. She teaches us about patience as we see trees grow slowly, and about being strong through different seasons. She shows us how nature is made up of many kinds of plants and animals, each special and unique, just like puzzle pieces. From the busy bees to the calm trees, each part is important, creating the big picture of our natural world.

Nature also teaches us to be kind and caring. When we take care of plants and animals, it's like giving a friend a hug or a smile when they need it. We learn to share, just like how animals and plants share their homes and food. By being good to nature, we learn to be good to each other, creating a world filled with kindness and love.

So, let's put on our explorer hats and dive into the amazing world of nature. Every leaf, rock, and animal is a new adventure waiting for us. Let's learn, look closely, and be amazed by the wonderful lessons Mother Earth has for us. Are you ready for this incredible adventure of learning and discovery, the curious Nature Explorer?

So, come on, let's put our boots on and go explore!

CHAPTER 20

THE DISCOVERY OF "NO": SETTING BOUNDARIES AND LEARNING CONSENT

You have learned thousands of new and exciting words ever since you could spell and read. But do you know the most important word you learned? Probably one of the first words you learned. A word that holds incredible power, the word "No." It might seem like a small word, but it's like a magic shield that helps you express what you feel inside and keeps yourself safe. Imagine it as a superhero word, strong and brave, ready to protect you whenever you need it. But I also need you to remember it is not about disrespect, it is about a world where everyone understands and respects this superhero word. Just like how you want others to listen when you say "no," it's important to listen and respect when someone else uses this powerful word. Being kind and understanding is like being a superhero with a heart full of empathy and care.

Using the word "no" nicely is an art, just like adding colors to a picture. It's about being gentle and thoughtful with your words. You can say, "No, thank you," to politely decline something. It's a way of being friendly and respectful while expressing your preferences and feelings. Now, let's imagine we have a magical "no" wand. With this wand, you can kindly say "no" in different situations. Whether it's a food you don't like, needing a break during playtime, or sharing your special toy, your "no" wand helps you communicate your thoughts and feelings in a nice way.

Practice using your "no" wand, and remember, you're not just using it for yourself; you're also learning to listen when others use it. You're becoming a superhero of kindness and understanding. So, keep working on this superpower of "no" and let it make your world a better and happier place.

Imagine yourself as the captain of your very own spaceship, exploring the vast universe. On your spaceship, you have a control panel with buttons and switches. Each button controls a part of your journey, and one of the most important buttons is the "No" button. This button helps you steer your spaceship in the right direction and make sure your journey is safe and enjoyable.

Being the captain of your spaceship means you get to decide where to go and how to get there. If someone suggests a route that doesn't feel right to you, pressing the "No" button is like saying, "Let's choose a different path." It's a way of setting boundaries and making decisions that are best for your space adventure.

Just like how you respect other planets and galaxies in the universe, it's important to respect each other's choices. If a fellow space traveler says "No" to doing something, it's their way of navigating their own journey. We should honor their choice, just like we'd want them to respect our decisions in this vast cosmic adventure.

Using your "No" button nicely is like communicating with other space explorers. You can say, "No, thank you," or "No, I'm not comfortable with that," to make sure everyone is on the same journey together. It's about creating a happy and harmonious space journey for everyone on board. The most important thing to remember is that you do not need to be rude to say no. You can always say no politely.

So, the next time you press the "No" button, imagine you're steering your spaceship through the stars, making choices that make your space adventure out of this world. Picture meeting an alien friend who can't speak like you do. They use funny moves and expressions to show what they like and don't like. It's like a dance of feelings! You learn to understand their "no" without words and show kindness in return.

In our big space family, we're all different. When someone uses their "no" code, it's like reading a map of their feelings. It's important to be a good space neighbor and respect their feelings, just like we'd want them to respect ours.

Imagine the "No" button in your spaceship as a reminder to be kind and listen to others. It's like a friendly flag waving in space, reminding us to understand and care for one another. As we keep flying through the stars, let's remember that every "no" helps us be better space buddies. It's like finding new stars that light up our friendship and make our journey among the galaxies even more amazing. Keep being a kind space explorer, understanding others, and making our cosmic adventure full of love and laughter...

Just like your favorite toy that you love to share with friends, understanding "no" is about sharing respect and kindness. When a space buddy uses their "no" code, it's like a little message saying, "I'm being true to myself." And just like how you love being yourself, you celebrate your friend for being true to them too!

It is like a big space party where everyone is invited. Some friends might say "no" to certain games or treats. That's okay! It's their way of saying what they like or don't like. We cheer for them and find something they'll enjoy because making everyone happy at the space party is our mission.

In our galaxy of friendship, we learn that "no" isn't about stopping fun. It's about making sure everyone feels comfortable and respected, just like arranging the planets in their right spots. Each "no" is like a little star that makes our galaxy even more incredible.

So, as we sail through the galaxy of friendship, let's celebrate the colors and stars that "no" brings. Let's keep understanding and respecting each other, making our space adventure the most amazing journey ever. Together, we'll create a galaxy filled with laughter, joy, and the magic of friendship.

CONCLUSION

Congratulations, young adventurers, on completing this incredible journey through *Essential Life Skills Every 9-Year-Old Needs to Know: A Guide to Help Young Boys and Girls Succeed in Life*. You've embarked on a magical quest, exploring the vast landscape of life's essential skills, learning valuable lessons, and unlocking the secrets to success. As we conclude this fun adventure, remember that each chapter you've explored is like a treasure chest filled with knowledge and wisdom. Just like a seasoned explorer, you now possess a treasure map that will guide you throughout your life's journey. From the importance of kindness and empathy to the power of perseverance and problem-solving, you've discovered the magical tools that will help you navigate the twists and turns of life. Your heart has been enriched with the spirit of gratitude, the joy of laughter, and the ability to turn challenges into triumphs. Life is a grand adventure, and you, dear adventurers, are now equipped with the essential life skills to brave its unpredictable waters.

Remember, you are the heroes of your own story, and each day is a new chapter waiting to be written.

SPECIAL BONUS

Want this bonus book for free?

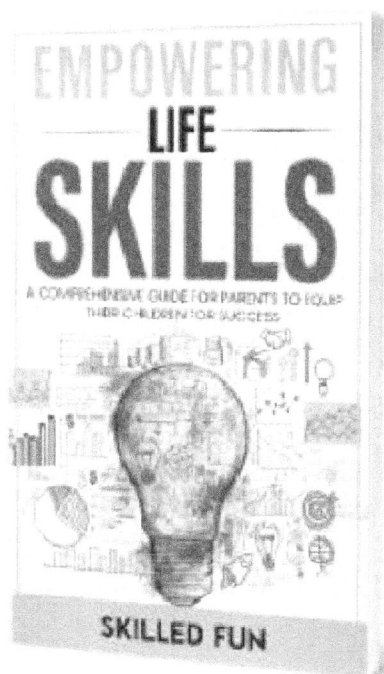

BONUS

FREE

SKILLED FUN

SKILLS and be the first to claim a free download of our upcoming releases.

Scan the QR CODE

Join Today!

THANK YOU

Thank you for choosing our resource to support your child's growth; it means so much to us.

If you could take a moment to share your thoughts on Amazon or Goodreads.com, it would mean a lot to us and be a great help to other parents searching for trusted resources. Thank you.

Want to dive into the literary world before anyone else? Then join our Book Launch Club! As a club member, you'll be offered the opportunity to receive advanced copies of our upcoming releases directly to your inbox. All we ask is for you to leave honest reviews on Amazon.com and Goodreads.com. Your honest feedback will contribute to the book's success and help fellow readers make informed choices.

For more information on joining Skilled Fun's Book Launch Club skilledfun.com/book-launch-club or simply scan our QR CODE

Made in United States
Orlando, FL
30 June 2025